ARAN
AFGHANS
TO CROCHET

If you love the romantic look of Aran pattern stitches, you should have this collection in your pattern library! Bonnie Marie Barker presents five full-size sampler afghans featuring a total of 5 gorgeous Aran patterns. To help you choose colors for your afghans, we're also showing the stitch patterns in a few popular hues. Create them for gifts, for home décor, or simply to enjoy for yourself. These lovely textures will yield a lifetime of warmth and beauty.

LEISURE ARTS, INC.
Maumelle, Arkansas

SAGE GREEN

Shown on front cover.

■■■□ **INTERMEDIATE**

Finished Size: 60" x 74", excluding fringe
(152.5 cm x 188 cm)

MATERIALS
Medium Weight Yarn [MEDIUM 4]
[7 ounces, 364 yards
(198 grams, 333 meters) per skein]:
12 skeins
Crochet hooks, sizes J (6 mm) **and** K (6.5 mm)
or sizes needed for gauge
Yarn needle

GAUGE: With smaller size hook,
20 sc = 6" (15 cm);
12 rows = 4" (10 cm)

Gauge Swatch: 6" x 4" (15 cm x 10 cm)
With smaller size hook, ch 21.
Row 1: Sc in second ch from hook and in each ch
across: 20 sc.
Rows 2-12: Ch 1, turn; sc in each sc across.
Finish off.

STITCH GUIDE

POPCORN (uses next st or sp)
Work 4 sc in st or sp indicated, drop loop from
hook, insert hook in first sc of 4-sc group, hook
dropped loop and draw through, ch 1 to close.

BACK POST DOUBLE CROCHET
(abbreviated BPdc)
YO, insert hook from **back** to **front** around post
of st indicated *(Fig. 3, page 26)*, YO and pull
up a loop even with last st made (3 loops on
hook), (YO and draw through 2 loops on hook)
twice. Skip st in front of BPdc.

BACK POST TREBLE CROCHET
(abbreviated BPtr)
YO twice, insert hook from **back** to **front** around
post of st indicated *(Fig. 3, page 26)*, YO and
pull up a loop even with last st made (4 loops on
hook), (YO and draw through 2 loops on hook)
3 times. Skip st in front of BPtr.

FRONT POST DOUBLE CROCHET
(abbreviated FPdc)
YO, insert hook from **front** to **back** around post
of st indicated *(Fig. 3, page 26)*, YO and pull
up a loop even with last st made (3 loops on
hook), (YO and draw through 2 loops on hook)
twice. Skip st behind FPdc.

FRONT POST TREBLE CROCHET
(abbreviated FPtr)
YO twice, insert hook from **front** to **back** around
post of st indicated *(Fig. 3, page 26)*, YO and
pull up a loop even with last st made (4 loops on
hook), (YO and draw through 2 loops on hook)
3 times. Skip st behind FPtr.

ch row is worked across length of Afghan.

rning chs are not included in st counts at the end
rows.

h smaller size hook, ch 248.

w 1 (Right side): Sc in second ch from hook and
each ch across: 247 sc.

te: Loop a short piece of yarn around any stitch
mark Row 1 as **right** side.

w 2: Ch 1, turn; skip first sc, sc in next sc and in
ch sc across, sc in turning ch.

w 3 (Low Ridge Front - first row): Turn; do **not**
p first sc, working in Front Loops Only **(Fig. 2,**
ge 26), slip st in each sc across, do **not** slip st in
ning ch.

w 4 (Low Ridge Front - second row): Ch 1, turn;
rking in free loops of sc on row **below (Fig. 1a,**
ge 26), sc in each st across.

w Ridge Front

w 5 (Cable - first row): Ch 1, turn; sc in first
★ ch 3, skip next 2 sc, sc in next sc, **turn**; sc
each ch of ch-3 just made, slip st in next sc (at
ginning of ch-3), **turn**; working **behind** ch-3, sc
2 skipped sc **(Figs. 5a-d, page 26)**; repeat from
cross, sc in turning ch: 82 Cables.

w 6 (Cable - second row): Ch 1, turn; skip first
and sc at base of cable, ★ working in **front** of
ble, 2 sc in next sc, sc in next sc, skip next sc
eginning of Cable); repeat from ★ across, sc in
ning ch: 247 sc.

able

Rows 7 and 8 (Low Ridge Front rows): Repeat
Rows 3 and 4.

Row 9 (Arrow - first row): Ch 2, turn; skip first
sc, dc in next sc, ★ skip next 3 sc, tr in next sc,
working **behind** tr just made, dc in 3 skipped sc;
repeat from ★ across to last sc, dc in last sc and in
turning ch.

Row 10 (Arrow - second row): Ch 2, turn; skip first
dc, dc in next dc, ★ skip next 3 dc, tr in next tr,
working in **front** of tr just made, dc in 3 skipped dc;
repeat from ★ across to last dc, dc in last dc and in
turning ch.

Arrow

Rows 11 and 12: Ch 1, turn; skip first st, sc in next
st and in each st across, sc in turning ch.

Rows 13-18: Repeat Rows 3-8.

Change to larger size hook.

Row 19 (Fisherman Popcorn - first row): Ch 1,
turn; skip first sc, sc in next sc, ★ ch 1, skip next sc,
work Popcorn in next sc, ch 1, skip next sc, sc in
next sc; repeat from ★ across to last sc, ch 1, skip
last sc, sc in turning ch: 61 Popcorns.

Row 20 (Fisherman Popcorn - second row): Ch 1,
turn; skip first sc, sc in next ch-1 sp, (ch 1, skip
next st, sc in next ch-1 sp) across to last st, ch 1,
skip last st, sc in turning ch.

Row 21 (Fisherman Popcorn - third row): Ch 1,
turn; skip first sc, work Popcorn in next ch-1 sp,
★ ch 1, skip next sc, sc in next ch-1 sp, ch 1, skip
next sc, work Popcorn in next ch-1 sp; repeat from
★ across to last sc, ch 1, skip last sc, sc in turning
ch: 62 Popcorns.

Row 22 (Fisherman Popcorn - fourth row): Repeat
Row 20.

Row 23 (Fisherman Popcorn - fifth row): Ch 1, turn; skip first sc, sc in next ch-1 sp, ★ ch 1, skip next sc, work Popcorn in next ch-1 sp, ch 1, skip next sc, sc in next ch-1 sp; repeat from ★ across to last sc, ch 1, skip last sc, sc in turning ch: 61 Popcorns.

Rows 24-41: Repeat Rows 20-23, 4 times; then repeat Rows 20 and 21 once **more**.

Fisherman Popcorn

Change to smaller size hook.

Row 42: Ch 1, turn; skip first sc, (2 sc in next ch-1 sp, skip next st) across, sc in turning ch: 247 sc.

Rows 43-48: Repeat Rows 3-8.

Row 49: Ch 1, turn; skip first sc, sc in next sc and in each sc across, sc in turning ch.

Row 50: Ch 1, do **not** turn; working from **left** to **right** in Front Loops Only, work reverse sc in each sc across *(Figs. 6a-d, page 27)*, slip st in turning ch.

Row 51: Ch 1, do **not** turn; working in free loops of sc on row **below**, sc in each sc across.

Rows 52 and 53: Repeat Rows 50 and 51.

Row 54: Ch 1, turn; skip first sc, sc in next sc and in each sc across, sc in turning ch.

Rows 55-60: Repeat Rows 3-8.

Row 61 (Celtic Weave - first row): Ch 2, turn; skip first sc, dc in next sc, ★ skip next 2 sc, tr in next 2 sc, working in **front** of 2 tr just made, tr in 2 skipped sc; repeat from ★ across to last dc, d in last dc and in turning ch.

Row 62 (Celtic Weave - second row): Ch 2, turn; skip first dc, work BPdc around next dc, work BP around each of next 2 sts, ★ skip next 2 sts, work BPtr around each of next 2 sts, working **behind** 2 sts just made, work BPtr around each of 2 skipp sts; repeat from ★ across to last 3 sts, work BPtr around each of next 2 sts, work BPdc around last dc in turning ch.

Row 63 (Celtic Weave - third row): Ch 2, turn; skip first dc, work FPdc around next BPdc, ★ skip next 2 BPtr, work FPtr around each of next 2 BPt working in **front** of 2 sts just made, work FPtr around each of 2 skipped sts; repeat from ★ across to last BPdc, FPdc around next BPdc, dc in turnin ch.

Rows 64-73: Repeat Rows 62 and 63, 5 times.

Celtic Weave

Row 74: Ch 2, turn; skip first dc, work BPdc arou each st across, dc in turning ch.

Rows 75-80: Repeat Rows 3-8.

...ws 81 and 82 (Shadowbox rows): Ch 2, turn; ...p first st, dc in next 4 sts, skip next 2 sts, tr ...ext 2 sts, working **behind** 2 tr just made, tr ...? skipped sts, skip next 2 sts, tr in next 2 sts, ...rking in **front** of 2 tr just made, tr in 2 skipped ...★ dc in next 2 sts, skip next 2 sts, tr in next ...s, working **behind** 2 tr just made, tr in 2 skipped ...skip next 2 sts, tr in next 2 sts, working in ...nt of 2 tr just made, tr in 2 skipped sts; repeat ...n ★ across to last 4 sts, dc in last 4 sts and in ...ning ch.

...adowbox

...ws 83 and 84: Ch 1, turn; skip first st, sc in next ...nd in each st across, sc in turning ch: 247 sc.

...ws 85-90: Repeat Rows 3-8.

...ws 91-104: Repeat Rows 61-74.

...ws 105-110: Repeat Rows 3-8.

Rows 111-116: Repeat Rows 49-54.

Rows 117-122: Repeat Rows 3-8.

Change to larger size hook.

Rows 123-146: Repeat Rows 19-42.

Rows 147-162: Repeat Rows 3-12 once, then repeat Rows 3-8 once **more**.

Row 163: Ch 1, turn; skip first sc, sc in next sc and in each sc across, sc in turning ch.

Do **not** finish off.

EDGING

Ch 1, turn; slip st in each sc across; working in end of rows, sc in first row, (ch 1, sc) 113 times evenly spaced across to next corner; working in free loops of beginning ch *(Fig. 1b, page 26)*, slip st in each ch across; working in end of rows, sc in first row, (ch 1, sc) 113 times evenly spaced across; join with slip st to first st, finish off.

FRINGE

Add fringe *(Figs. 7a-c, page 27)* in first ch-1 sp and in every other ch-1 sp across each end.

BASKETWEAVE

Finished Size: 65" x 69", excluding fringe
(165 cm x 175 cm)

MATERIALS

Medium Weight Yarn **MEDIUM 4**
    [7 ounces, 364 yards
    (198 grams, 333 meters) per skein**]:**
    12 skeins
Crochet hook, size I (5.5 mm) **or** size needed for
    gauge
Yarn needle

GAUGE: 14 sc and 16 rows = 4" (10 cm)

Gauge Swatch: 4" square (10 cm)
With smaller size hook, ch 15.
Row 1: Sc in second ch from hook and in each ch
across: 14 sc.
Rows 2-16: Ch 1, turn; sc in each sc across.
Finish off.

STITCH GUIDE

BACK POST DOUBLE CROCHET
    (abbreviated BPdc)
YO, insert hook from **back** to **front** around po
of st indicated *(Fig. 3, page 26)*, YO and pull
up a loop even with last st made (3 loops on
hook), (YO and draw through 2 loops on hook)
twice. Skip st in front of BPdc.

FRONT POST DOUBLE CROCHET
    (abbreviated FPdc)
YO, insert hook from **front** to **back** around po
of st indicated *(Fig. 3, page 26)*, YO and pull
up a loop even with last st made (3 loops on
hook), (YO and draw through 2 loops on hook)
twice. Skip st behind FPdc.

Each row is worked across length of Afghan.

Turning chs are not included in st counts at the end of rows.

Ch 242.

Row 1 (Right side): Sc in second ch from hook and in each ch across: 241 sc.

Note: Loop a short piece of yarn around any stitch to mark Row 1 as **right** side.

Row 2: Ch 1, turn; skip first sc, sc in next sc and in each sc across, sc in turning ch.

Row 3 (Low Ridge Front – first row): Turn; do **not** skip first sc, working in front loops only *(Fig. 2, page 26)*, slip st in each sc across, do **not** slip st in turning ch.

Row 4 (Low Ridge Front – second row): Ch 1, turn; working in free loops of row **below** *(Fig. 1a, page 26)*, sc in each st across.

Low Ridge Front

Row 5 (Cable – first row): Ch 1, turn; sc in first sc, ★ ch 3, skip next 2 sc, sc in next sc, **turn**; sc in each ch of ch-3 just made, slip st in next sc (at beginning of ch-3), **turn**; working **behind** ch-3, sc in 2 skipped sc *(Figs. 5a-d, page 26)*; repeat from ★ across, sc in turning ch: 80 Cables.

Row 6 (Cable – second row): Ch 1, turn; skip first sc and sc at base of cable, ★ working in **front** of cable, 2 sc in next sc, sc in next sc, skip next sc (beginning of cable); repeat from ★ across, sc in turning ch: 241 sc.

Cable

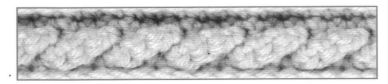

Rows 7 and 8 (Low Ridge Front rows): Repeat Rows 3 and 4.

Row 9 (Arrow – first row): Ch 2, turn; dc in first ★ skip next 3 sc, tr in next sc, working **behind** tr just made, dc in 3 skipped sc; repeat from ★ acro dc in turning ch: 242 sts.

Row 10 (Arrow – second row): Ch 2, turn; skip f 4 dc, tr in next tr, working in **front** of tr just mad dc in last 3 skipped dc, ★ skip next 3 dc, tr in nex tr, working in **front** of tr just made, dc in 3 skipp dc; repeat from ★ across to last dc, dc in last dc a in turning ch.

Arrow

Row 11: Ch 1, turn; skip first st, sc in next st and each st across, sc in turning ch: 242 sc.

Row 12: Ch 1, turn; skip first sc, sc in next sc an in each sc across, do **not** sc in turning ch: 241 sc

Rows 13-18: Repeat Rows 3-8.

Row 19 (Basketweave – first row): Ch 2, turn; sl first st, ★ work BPdc around each of next 3 sts, work FPdc around each of next 3 sts; repeat from across, hdc in turning ch.

Rows 20 and 21 (Basketweave – second and third rows): Ch 2, turn; skip first hdc, ★ work BP around each of next 3 sts, work FPdc around eac of next 3 sts; repeat from ★ across, hdc in turning

Rows 22-24 (Basketweave – fourth thru sixth rows): Ch 2, turn; skip first hdc, ★ work FPdc around each of next 3 sts, work BPdc around eac of next 3 sts; repeat from ★ across, hdc in turning

Rows 25-42: Repeat Rows 19-24, 3 times.

Basketweave

Row 43: Ch 1, turn; skip first st, sc in next st and in ch st across, sc in turning ch.

Row 44 (Low Ridge Back – first row)**:** Turn; do **not** skip first sc, working in back loops only, slip st in ch sc across, do **not** slip st in turning ch.

Row 45 (Low Ridge Back – second row)**:** Ch 1, turn; working in free loops of sc on row **below**, sc in ch st across.

Low Ridge Back

Row 46: Ch 1, turn; skip first sc, sc in each sc across, sc in turning ch.

Rows 47 and 48 (Cable rows)**:** Repeat Rows 5 and 6.

Rows 49 and 50 (Low Ridge Front rows)**:** Repeat Rows 3 and 4.

Row 51: Ch 1, turn; skip first sc, sc in next sc and in each sc across, sc in turning ch.

Row 52: Ch 1, do **not** turn; working from **left** to **right** in front loops only, work reverse sc in each sc across *(Figs. 6a-d, page 27)*, slip st in turning ch.

Row 53: Ch 1, do **not** turn; working in free loops of sc on row **below**, sc in each sc across.

Rows 54 and 55: Repeat Rows 52 and 53.

Row 56: Ch 1, turn; skip first sc, sc in next sc and in each sc across, sc in turning ch.

Rows 57-62: Repeat Rows 3-8.

Rows 63-90: Repeat Rows 19-46.

Rows 91-94: Repeat Rows 5-8.

Shadowbox

Rows 95 and 96 (Shadowbox rows)**:** Ch 2, turn; skip first st, dc in next st, skip next 2 sts, tr in next 2 sts, working **behind** 2 tr just made, tr in 2 skipped sts, skip next 2 sts, tr in next 2 sts, working in **front** of 2 tr just made, tr in 2 skipped sts, ★ dc in next 2 sts, skip next 2 sts, tr in next 2 sts, working **behind** 2 tr just made, tr in 2 skipped sts, skip next 2 sts, tr in next 2 sts, working in **front** of 2 tr just made, tr in 2 skipped sts; repeat from ★ across to last st, dc in last st and in turning ch.

Rows 97-100: Repeat Rows 43-46.

Rows 101-104: Repeat Rows 5-8.

Rows 105-148: Repeat Rows 19-62.

Rows 149-172: Repeat 19-42.

Rows 173 and 174: Ch 1, turn; skip first sc, sc in next sc and in each sc across, sc in turning ch.

Rows 175-190: Repeat Rows 3-18.

Row 191: Ch 1, turn; skip first sc, sc in next sc and in each sc across, sc in turning ch; do **not** finish off.

EDGING

Ch 1, working from **left** to **right**, work reverse sc in each sc across last row; turn afghan so that **wrong** side is facing; working in end of rows, sc in first row, (ch 1, sc) 127 times evenly spaced across to next corner; turn Afghan so that **right** side is facing; working in free loops of beginning ch *(Fig. 1b, page 26)*, work reverse sc in each ch across; turn afghan so that **wrong** side is facing; working in end of rows, sc in first row, (ch 1, sc) 127 times evenly spaced across; join with slip st to first st, finish off.

FRINGE

Add fringe *(Figs. 7a-c, page 27)* in first ch-1 sp and in every other ch-1 sp across each end.

TAN SAMPLER

Shown on back cover.

■■■□ **INTERMEDIATE**

Finished Size: 59½" x 76", excluding fringe
(151 cm x 193 cm)

MATERIALS

Medium Weight Yarn
[7 ounces, 364 yards
(198 grams, 333 meters) per skein]:
11 skeins
Crochet hook, size I (5.5 mm) **or** size needed for
gauge
Stitch markers
Yarn needle

GAUGE: 14 sc and 16 rows = 4" (10 cm)

Gauge Swatch: 4" square (10 cm)
Ch 15.
Row 1: Sc in second ch from hook and in each ch
across: 14 sc.
Rows 2-16: Ch 1, turn; sc in each sc across.
Finish off.

STITCH GUIDE

BACK POST DOUBLE CROCHET
(abbreviated BPdc)
YO, insert hook from **back** to **front** around post
of st indicated *(Fig. 3, page 26)*, YO and pull
up a loop even with last st made (3 loops on
hook), (YO and draw through 2 loops on hook)
twice. Skip st in front of BPdc.

FRONT POST DOUBLE CROCHET
(abbreviated FPdc)
YO, insert hook from **front** to **back** around post
of st indicated *(Fig. 3, page 26)*, YO and pull
up a loop even with last st made (3 loops on
hook), (YO and draw through 2 loops on hook)
twice. Skip st behind FPdc.

WOVEN STITCH
(abbreviated Woven St)
YO, insert hook in st indicated, YO and pull up
a loop through st and one loop on hook, YO and
draw through 2 loops on hook, YO, insert hook
same st and pull up a loop through st and both
loops on hook.

QUARE (Make 30)

39.

ow 1 (Right side): Dc in third ch from hook and in
ch ch across: 37 dc.

ote: Loop a short piece of yarn around any stitch
mark Row 1 as **right** side.

ow 2 (Basketweave – first row): Ch 2, turn; skip
st st, ★ work BPdc around each of next 3 sts,
ork FPdc around each of next 3 sts; repeat from ★
cross, hdc in turning ch.

ows 3 and 4 (Basketweave – second and third
ows): Ch 2, turn; skip first hdc, ★ work BPdc
round each of next 3 sts, work FPdc around each
f next 3 sts; repeat from ★ across, hdc in turning ch.

ows 5-7 (Basketweave – fourth thru sixth rows):
h 2, turn; skip first hdc, ★ work FPdc around each
f next 3 sts, work BPdc around each of next 3 sts;
epeat from ★ across, hdc in turning ch.

ows 8-13: Repeat Rows 2-7.

asketweave

Row 14: Ch 1, turn; skip first st, sc in next st and in
each st across, sc in turning ch.

Row 15 (Low Ridge Front – first row): Turn, do
not skip first sc; working in Front Loops Only
(Fig. 2, page 26), slip st in each sc across, do **not**
slip st in turning ch.

Row 16 (Low Ridge Front – second row): Ch 1,
turn; working in free loops of sc on row **below**
(Fig. 1a, page 26), sc in each sc across.

Low Ridge Front

Row 17: Ch 1, turn; skip first st, sc in next sc and in
each st across, sc in turning ch.

Row 18: Ch 1, do **not** turn; working from **left**
to **right** in Front Loops Only, work reverse sc in
each sc across **(Figs. 6a-d, page 27)**, slip st in
turning ch.

Row 19: Ch 1, do **not** turn; working in free loops of
sc on row **below**, sc in each sc across.

Rows 20 and 21: Repeat Rows 18 and 19.

Row 22: Ch 1, turn; skip first st, sc in next sc and in
each st across, sc in turning ch.

Rows 23 and 24 (Low Ridge Front rows): Repeat
Rows 15 and 16.

Row 25 (Cable – first row): Ch 1, turn; sc in first
sc, ★ ch 3, skip next 2 sc, sc in next sc, **turn**; sc
in each ch of ch-3 just made, slip st in next sc (at
beginning of ch-3), **turn**; working **behind** ch-3, sc
in 2 skipped sc **(Figs. 5a-d, page 26)**; repeat from
★ across, sc in turning ch: 12 Cables.

Row 26 (Cable – second row): Ch 1, turn; skip
first sc and sc at base of cable, ★ working in **front**
of cable, 2 sc in next sc, sc in next sc, skip next sc
(beginning of cable); repeat from ★ across, sc in
turning ch: 37 sc.

Cable

Rows 27 and 28 (Low Ridge Front rows): Repeat Rows 15 and 16.

Row 29 (Arrow – first row): Ch 2, turn; dc in first sc, ★ skip next 3 sc, tr in next sc, working **behind** tr just made, dc in 3 skipped sc; repeat from ★ across, dc in turning ch: 38 sts.

Row 30 (Arrow – second row): Ch 2, turn; skip first 4 dc, tr in next tr, working in **front** of tr just made, dc in last 3 skipped dc, ★ skip next 3 dc, tr in next tr, working in **front** of tr just made, dc in 3 skipped dc; repeat from ★ across to last dc, dc in last dc: 37 sts.

Arrow

Rows 31-36: Repeat Rows 23-28.

Do **not** finish off.

SQUARE EDGING
Ch 1, turn; sc in first st and in each sc across, sc in turning ch, mark last st for corner; working in end of rows, work 38 sc evenly spaced across to next corner, mark last st for corner; working in free loops of beginning ch *(Fig. 1b, page 26)*, sc in each ch across, mark last st for corner; working in end of rows, work 38 sc evenly spaced across to next corner, mark last st for corner; join with slip st to first sc, finish off: 152 sc.

ASSEMBLY
Referring to Assembly Diagram, page 13, for directional placement of Squares, hold 2 Squares with **wrong** sides together; working through **both** loops of **both** thicknesses, join yarn with slip st in top left marked corner st on **front Square** and in st to **right** of marked st on **back Square**; ch 1, working from **left** to **right**, work reverse sc in each sc across, ending in marked st on **back Square**; finish off. Continue joining Squares in same manner, forming 5 vertical strips of 6 Squares each, then join strips in same manner.

EDGING
With **right** side facing, join yarn with slip st in top right corner; ch 1, ★ sc in each sc across to next corner; turn Afghan so **wrong** side is facing, work reverse sc in each st across long edge to next corner; turn Afghan so **right** side is facing; repeat from ★ once **more**; join with slip st to first sc, do **not** finish off.

FIRST END
Row 1: Ch 2, skip first sc, work Woven St in next sc, ★ skip next sc, work Woven St in next sc; repeat from ★ across to corner.

Rows 2-9: Ch 2, turn; skip first Woven St, work Woven St in sp **before** next Woven St and in sp **before** each Woven St across *(Fig. 4, page 26)*, work Woven St in sp **before** turning ch.

Finish off.

SECOND END
With **right** side facing, join yarn with slip st in first sc on opposite end. Complete same as First End.

FINISHING
Add fringe *(Figs. 7a-c, page 27)* in sp between first 2 Woven Sts and in sp before every other Woven St across each end.

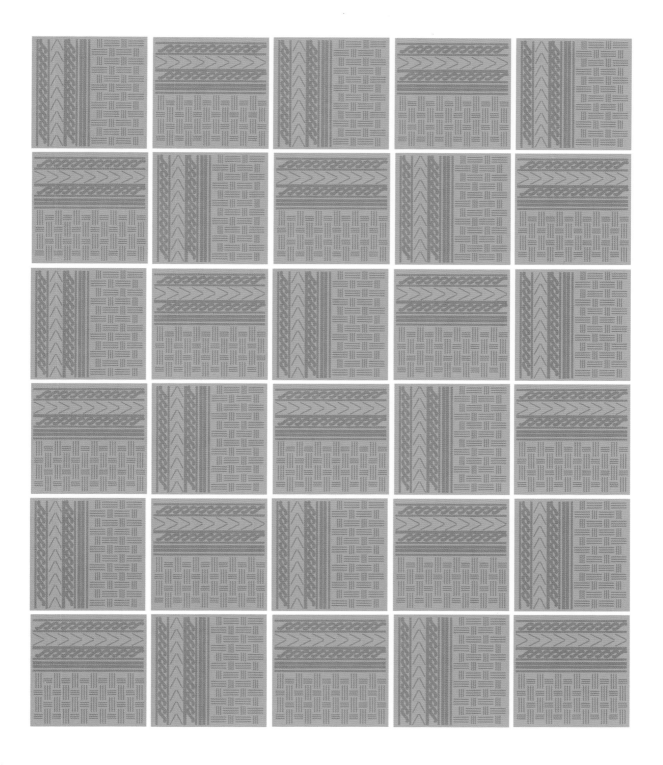

WINTER WHITE

Finished Size: 64½" x 59½", excluding fringe
(164 cm x 151 cm)

MATERIALS
Medium Weight Yarn
[7 ounces, 364 yards
(198 grams, 333 meters) per skein]:
10 skeins
Crochet hooks, sizes J (6 mm) **and** K (6.5 mm)
or sizes needed for gauge
Yarn needle

GAUGE: With smaller size hook,
20 sc = 6" (15 cm) and
12 rows = 4" (10 cm)

Gauge Swatch: 6" x 4" (15 cm x 10 cm)
With smaller size hook, ch 21.
Row 1: Sc in second ch from hook and in each ch
across: 20 sc.
Rows 2-12: Ch 1, turn; sc in each sc across.
Finish off.

STITCH GUIDE
POPCORN (uses next st or sp)
Work 4 sc in st or sp indicated, drop loop from
hook, insert hook in first sc of 4-sc group, hook
dropped loop and draw through, ch 1 to close.

FRONT POST TREBLE CROCHET
(abbreviated FPtr)
YO twice, insert hook from **front** to **back**
(Fig. 3, page 26) around post of sc indicated,
YO and pull up a loop even with st on
hook(4 loops on hook), (YO and draw through
2 loops on hook) 3 times.

Each row is worked across length of Afghan.

Turning chs are not included in st counts at the e
of rows.

With smaller size hook, ch 197.

Row 1 (Right side)**:** Sc in second ch from hook a
in each ch across: 196 sc.

Note: Loop a short piece of yarn around any stitc
to mark Row 1 as **right** side.

Rows 2 and 3: Ch 1, turn; skip first sc, sc in next
and in each sc across, sc in turning ch.

Row 4 (Low Ridge Back - first row)**:** Turn; do **no**
skip first st, working in back loops only *(Fig. 2,
page 26)*, slip st in each st across, do **not** slip st
turning ch.

Row 5 (Low Ridge Back - second row)**:** Ch 1, tur
working in free loops of sc on row **below** *(Fig. 1
page 26)*, sc in each sc across.

Low Ridge Back

Row 6: Ch 1, turn; skip first sc, sc in next sc and
each sc across, sc in turning ch.

Row 7 (Cable - first row)**:** Ch 1, turn; sc in first
sc, ★ ch 3, skip next 2 sc, sc in next sc, **turn**; sc
in each ch of ch-3 just made, slip st in next sc (at
beginning of ch-3), **turn**; working **behind** ch-3, s
in 2 skipped sc *(Figs. 5a-d, page 26)*; repeat fr
★ across, sc in turning ch: 65 Cables.

Row 8 (Cable - second row): Ch 1, turn; skip first sc and sc at base of cable, ★ working in **front** of cable, 2 sc in next sc, sc in next sc, skip next sc (beginning of cable); repeat from ★ across, sc in turning ch: 196 sc.

Cable

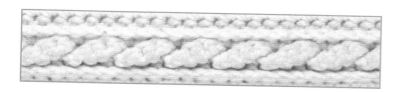

Row 9: Ch 1, turn; skip first sc, sc in next sc and in each sc across, sc in turning ch.

Rows 10 and 11 (Low Ridge Back rows): Repeat Rows 4 and 5.

Row 12: Ch 1, turn; sc in first sc and in each sc across, sc in turning ch: 197 sts.

Row 13 (Arrow - first row): Ch 2, turn; skip first 4 sc, tr in next sc, working **behind** tr just made, dc in last 3 skipped sc, ★ skip next 3 sc, tr in next sc, working **behind** tr just made, dc in 3 skipped sc; repeat from ★ across, dc in turning ch.

Row 14 (Arrow - second row): Ch 2, turn; skip first 4 dc, tr in next tr, working in **front** of tr just made, dc in last 3 skipped dc, ★ skip next 3 dc, tr in next tr, working in **front** of tr just made, dc in 3 skipped dc; repeat from ★ across, dc in turning ch.

Arrow

Row 15: Ch 1, turn; skip first st, sc in next st and in each st across, sc in turning ch: 197 sc.

Row 16: Ch 1, turn; skip first sc, sc in next sc and in each sc across, do **not** sc in turning ch: 196 sc.

Row 17 (Low Ridge Front - first row): Turn; do **not** skip first sc, working in front loops only, slip st in next st and in each st across, do **not** slip st in turning ch.

Row 18 (Low Ridge Front - second row): Ch 1, turn; working in free loops of row **below**, sc in eac st across.

Low Ridge Front

Rows 19 and 20 (Cable rows): Repeat Rows 7 and 8.

Rows 21 and 22 (Low Ridge Front rows): Repeat Rows 17 and 18.

Rows 23 and 24: Ch 1, turn; skip first sc, sc in nex sc and in each sc across, sc in turning ch.

Row 25 (Diamonds - first row): Ch 1, turn; skip first sc, sc in next 2 sc, working in **front** of sts, wor FPtr around second sc in Row 22, ★ skip next 4 sc on Row 22, work FPtr around next sc, skip 2 sc behind FPtr, sc in next 4 sc, work FPtr around s next to last FPtr made; repeat from ★ across to last sc, skip sc behind FPtr, sc in turning ch.

Rows 26-28: Ch 1, turn; skip first sc, sc in next st and in each st across, sc in turning ch.

Row 29 (Diamonds - fifth row): Ch 1, turn; skip first 3 sc 2 rows **below**, working in **front** of sts, work FPtr around next sc, skip sc behind FPtr, ★ sc in next 4 sc, work FPtr around sc next to last FPtr made, skip next 4 sc 2 rows **below**, work FPtr around next sc; repeat from ★ across to last 4 sc, skip 2 sc behind FPtr, sc in next 2 sc and in turning ch.

Rows 30-32: Ch 1, turn; skip first sc, sc in next st and in each st across, sc in turning ch.

Row 33 (Diamonds - ninth row): Ch 1, turn; skip first sc, sc in next 2 sc, working in **front** of sts, work FPtr around second sc 2 rows **below**, ★ skip next 4 sc on Row 31, work FPtr around next sc, skip 2 sc behind FPtr, sc in next 4 sc, work FPtr around sc next to last FPtr made; repeat from ★ across to last sc, skip sc behind FPtr, sc in turning ch.

Rows 34-54: Repeat Rows 26-33 twice, then repeat Rows 26-30 once **more**.

Diamond Pattern

Row 55 (Low Ridge Front - first row): Turn; do **not** [ski]p first sc, working in Front Loops Only, slip st [in] next st and in each st across, do **not** slip st in [tur]ning ch.

Row 56 (Low Ridge Front - second row): Ch 1, [tur]n; working in free loops of sc on row **below**, sc in [eac]h sc across.

Rows 57 and 58 (Cable rows): Repeat Rows 7 and 8.

Rows 59 and 60 (Low Ridge Front rows): Repeat [Ro]ws 55 and 56.

Row 61: Ch 1, turn; skip first st, sc in next st and in [eac]h st across, sc in turning ch.

Row 62: Ch 1, do **not** turn; working from **left** [to] **right** in Front Loops Only, work reverse sc in [eac]h sc across *(Figs. 6a-d, page 27)*, slip st in [tur]ning ch.

Row 63: Ch 1, do **not** turn; working in free loops of [sc] on row **below**, sc in each sc across.

Rows 64 and 65: Repeat Rows 62 and 63.

Row 66: Ch 1, turn; skip first sc, sc in next sc and [in] each sc across, sc in turning ch.

Rows 67-72: Repeat Rows 55-60.

[Ch]ange to larger size hook.

Row 73 (Fisherman Popcorn - first row): Ch 1, [tur]n; sc in first sc, ch 1, skip next sc, work Popcorn [in n]ext sc, ★ ch 1, skip next sc, sc in next sc, ch 1, [ski]p next sc, work Popcorn in next sc; repeat from ★ [a]cross to last st, ch 1, skip last sc, sc in turning [ch:] 49 Popcorns.

Row 74 (Fisherman Popcorn - second row): Ch 1, turn; skip first sc, sc in next ch-1 sp, (ch 1, skip next st, sc in next ch-1 sp) across to last st, ch 1, skip last st, sc in turning ch.

Row 75 (Fisherman Popcorn - third row): Ch 1, turn; skip first sc, work Popcorn in next ch-1 sp, ch 1, skip next sc, sc in next ch-1 sp, ★ ch 1, skip next sc, work Popcorn in next ch-1 sp, ch 1, skip next sc, sc in next ch-1 sp; repeat from ★ across to last sc, ch 1, skip last sc, sc in turning ch: 49 Popcorns.

Row 76 (Fisherman Popcorn - fourth row): Repeat Row 74.

Row 77 (Fisherman Popcorn - fifth row): Ch 1, turn; skip first sc, sc in next ch-1 sp, ch 1, skip next sc, work Popcorn in next ch-1 sp, ★ ch 1, skip next sc, sc in next ch-1 sp, ch 1, skip next sc, work Popcorn in next ch-1 sp; repeat from ★ across to last sc, ch 1, skip last sc, sc in turning ch.

Rows 78-95: Repeat Rows 74-77, 4 times; then repeat Rows 74 and 75 once **more**.

Fisherman Popcorn

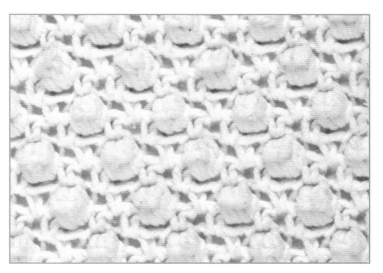

Change to smaller size hook.

Row 96: Ch 1, turn; skip first st, sc in next st and in each st and each ch-1 sp across, do **not** sc in turning ch: 196 sc.

Rows 97-102: Repeat Rows 55-60.

Row 103 (Popcorn Diamond - first row): Ch 1, turn; sc in first 6 sc, work Popcorn in next sc, ★ sc in next 7 sc, work Popcorn in next sc; repeat from ★ across to last 5 sc, sc in last 5 sc and in turning ch: 24 Popcorns.

Row 104 (Popcorn Diamond - second row): Ch 1, turn; skip first st, sc in next st and in each st across, sc in turning ch.

Row 105 (Popcorn Diamond - third row): Ch 1, turn; skip first sc, sc in next 4 sc, ★ work Popcorn in next sc, sc in next 3 sc; repeat from ★ across, sc in turning ch: 48 Popcorns.

Row 106: Repeat Row 104.

Row 107 (Popcorn Diamond - fifth row): Ch 1, turn; skip first sc, sc in next 3 sc, work Popcorn in next sc, sc in next 5 sc, work Popcorn in next sc, ★ sc in next sc, work Popcorn in next sc, sc in next 5 sc, work Popcorn in next sc; repeat from ★ across to last 2 sc, sc in last 2 sc and in turning ch.

Rows 108-110: Repeat Rows 104 and 105, then repeat Row 104 once **more**.

Row 111 (Popcorn Diamond - ninth row): Ch 1, turn; skip first sc, sc in next 6 sc, work Popcorn in next sc, ★ sc in next 7 sc, work Popcorn in next sc; repeat from ★ across to last 5 sc, sc in last 5 sc and in turning ch.

Row 112 (Popcorn Diamond - last row): Ch 1, turn; skip first st, sc in next st and in each st across, do **not** sc in turning ch: 196 sc.

Popcorn Diamond

Rows 113-142: Repeat Rows 67-96.

Rows 143-160: Repeat Rows 55-72.

Rows 161-190: Repeat Rows 25-54.

Rows 191-197: Repeat Rows 55-61.

Row 198: Ch 1, turn; sc in first sc and in each sc across, sc in turning ch: 197 sc.

Rows 199 and 200 (Arrow rows): Repeat Rows 13 and 14.

Row 201: Ch 1, turn; skip first st, sc in next st and in each st across, sc in turning ch.

Row 202: Ch 1, turn; skip first st, sc in next st and in each st across, do **not** sc in turning ch: 196 sc.

Rows 203-208: Repeat Rows 55-60.

Rows 209 and 210: Ch 1, turn; skip first st, sc in next st and in each st across, sc in turning ch.

Do **not** finish off.

EDGING
Ch 1, turn; slip st in each sc across; working in end of rows, sc in first row, (ch 1, sc) 107 times evenly spaced across to next corner; working in free loop of beginning ch *(Fig. 1b, page 26)*, slip st in each ch across; working in end of rows, sc in first row, (ch 1, sc) 107 times evenly spaced across; join with slip st to first st, finish off.

FRINGE
Add fringe *(Figs. 7a-c, page 27)* in first ch-1 sp and in every other ch-1 sp across each end.

AUTUMN ORANGE

own on page 21.

ished Size: 62½" x 60", excluding fringe
(159 cm : 5 cm)

MEDIUM 4

ATERIALS
Medium Weight Yarn
    [7 ounces, 364 yards
    (198 grams, 333 meters) per skein]:
    12 skeins
Crochet hooks, sizes I (5.5 mm) **and** J (6 mm) **or**
    sizes needed for gauge
Yarn needle

AUGE: With smaller size hook,
        14 sc and 16 rows = 4" (10 cm)

auge Swatch: 4" square (10 cm)
th smaller size hook, ch 15.
w 1: Sc in second ch from hook and in each ch
oss: 14 sc.
ws 2-16: Ch 1, turn; sc in each sc across.
nish off.

STITCH GUIDE

POPCORN (uses next st or sp)
Work 4 sc in st or sp indicated, drop loop from hook, insert hook in first sc of 4-sc group, hook dropped loop and draw through, ch 1 to close.

BACK POST TREBLE CROCHET (abbreviated BPtr)
YO twice, insert hook from **back** to **front** around post of st indicated *(Fig. 3, page 26)*, YO and pull up a loop even with last st made (4 loops on hook), (YO and draw through 2 loops on hook) 3 times. Skip st in front of BPtr.

BACK POST DOUBLE CROCHET (abbreviated BPdc)
YO, insert hook from **back** to **front** around post of st indicated *(Fig. 3, page 26)*, YO and pull up a loop even with last st made (3 loops on hook), (YO and draw through 2 loops on hook) twice. Skip st in front of BPdc.

FRONT POST DOUBLE CROCHET (abbreviated FPdc)
YO, insert hook from **front** to **back** around post of st indicated *(Fig. 3, page 26)*, YO and pull up a loop even with last st made (3 loops on hook), (YO and draw through 2 loops on hook) twice. Skip st behind FPdc.

FRONT POST TREBLE CROCHET (abbreviated FPtr)
YO twice, insert hook from **front** to **back** around post of st indicated *(Fig. 3, page 26)*, YO and pull up a loop even with last st made (4 loops on hook), (YO and draw through 2 loops on hook) 3 times. Skip st behind FPtr.

Each row is worked across length of Afghan.

Turning chs are not included in st counts at the end of rows.

With smaller size hook, ch 208.

Row 1 (Right side): Sc in second ch from hook and in each ch across: 207 sc.

Note: Loop a short piece of yarn through any stitch to mark Row 1 as **right** side.

Row 2: Ch 1, turn; skip first sc, sc in next sc and in each sc across, sc in turning ch.

Row 3 (Low Ridge Front - first row): Turn; do **not** skip first sc, working in Front Loops Only *(Fig. 2, page 26)*, slip st in each sc across, do **not** slip st in turning ch.

Row 4 (Low Ridge Front - second row): Ch 1, turn; working in free loops of sc on row **below** *(Fig. 1a, page 26)*, sc in each sc across.

Low Ridge Front

Row 5 (Arrow - first row): Ch 2, turn; skip first sc, dc in next sc, ★ skip next 3 sc, tr in next sc, working **behind** tr just made, dc in 3 skipped sc; repeat from ★ across to last sc, dc in last sc, do **not** work in turning ch: 206 sts.

Row 6 (Arrow - second row): Ch 2, turn; skip first 4 dc, tr in next tr, working in **front** of tr just made, dc in last 3 skipped dc, ★ skip next 3 dc, tr in next tr, working in **front** of tr just made, dc in 3 skipped dc; repeat from ★ across to last dc, dc in last dc and in turning ch.

Arrow

Rows 7 and 8: Ch 1, turn; skip first st, sc in next st and in each st across, sc in turning ch.

Rows 9 and 10: Repeat Rows 3 and 4.

Change to larger size hook.

Row 11 (Fisherman Popcorn - first row): Ch 1, turn; skip first sc, sc in next sc, ★ ch 1, skip next sc, work Popcorn in next sc, ch 1, skip next sc, sc in next sc; repeat from ★ across; do **not** work in turning ch: 51 Popcorns.

Row 12 (Fisherman Popcorn - second row): Ch 1 turn; skip first sc, sc in next ch-1 sp, (ch 1, skip next st, sc in next ch-1 sp) across to last sc, ch 1, skip last sc, sc in turning ch.

Row 13 (Fisherman Popcorn - third row): Ch 1, turn; skip first sc, work Popcorn in next ch-1 sp, ch 1, skip next sc, sc in next ch-1 sp, ★ ch 1, skip next sc, work Popcorn in next ch-1 sp, ch 1, skip next sc, sc in next ch-1 sp; repeat from ★ across to last sc, ch 1, skip last sc, work Popcorn in turning ch: 52 Popcorns.

Row 14 (Fisherman Popcorn - fourth row): Repe Row 12.

Row 15 (Fisherman Popcorn - fifth row): Ch 1, turn; skip first sc, sc in next ch-1 sp, ch 1, skip next sc, work Popcorn in next ch-1 sp, ★ ch 1, skip next sc, sc in next ch-1 sp, ch 1, skip next sc, wor Popcorn in next ch-1 sp; repeat from ★ across to last sc, ch 1, skip last sc, sc in turning ch: 51 Popcorns.

Rows 16-25: Repeat Rows 12-15 twice, then repe Rows 12 and 13 once **more**.

Change to smaller size hook.

Row 26: Ch 1, turn; sc in first Popcorn, (2 sc in next ch-1 sp, skip next st) across to last Popcorn, skip last Popcorn, 2 sc in turning ch: 207 sc.

Fisherman Popcorn

Rows 27-34: Repeat Rows 3-10.

Row 35 (Celtic Weave - first row)**:** Ch 2, turn; skip first sc, dc in next sc, ★ skip next 2 sc, tr in next 2 sc, working in **front** of 2 tr just made, tr in 2 skipped sc; repeat from ★ across, dc in turning ch.

Row 36 (Celtic Weave - second row)**:** Ch 2, turn; skip first st, work BPtr around each of next 2 sts, ★ skip next 2 sts, work BPtr around each of next 2 sts, working **behind** 2 sts just made, work BPtr around each of 2 skipped sts; repeat from ★ across to last 3 sts, work BPtr around each of next 2 sts, work BPdc around last st, dc in turning ch.

Row 37 (Celtic Weave - third row)**:** Ch 2, turn; skip first dc, work FPdc around next BPdc, ★ skip next 2 BPtr, work FPtr around each of next 2 BPtr, working in **front** of 2 sts just made, work FPtr around each of 2 skipped sts; repeat from ★ across, dc in turning ch.

Rows 38-42: Repeat Rows 36 and 37 twice, then repeat Row 36 once **more**.

Celtic Weave

Row 43: Ch 2, turn; skip first dc, work FPdc around each st across, dc in turning ch.

Row 44: Ch 1, turn; sc in first st and in each st across, sc in turning ch: 207 sc.

Rows 45-76: Repeat Rows 3-34.

Row 77 (Celtic Diamond - first row)**:** Ch 2, turn; skip first sc, dc in next 10 sc, skip next 2 sc, tr in next 2 sc, working in **front** of 2 tr just made, tr in 2 skipped sc, ★ dc in next 14 sc, skip next 2 sc, in next 2 sc, working in **front** of 2 tr just made, tr 2 skipped tr; repeat from ★ 9 times **more**, dc in la 11 dc and in turning ch.

Row 78 (Celtic Diamond - second row)**:** Ch 2, tur skip first dc, dc in next 9 sts, [skip next 2 sts, wor BPtr around each of next 2 sts, working **behind** 2 sts just made, work BPtr around each of 2 skipp sts] twice, ★ dc in next 10 sts, [skip next 2 sts, wo BPtr around each of next 2 sts, working **behind** 2 sts just made, work BPtr around each of 2 skipp sts] twice; repeat from ★ 9 times **more**, dc in last 8 sts and in turning ch.

Row 79 (Celtic Diamond - third row)**:** Ch 2, turn; skip first dc, dc in next 6 sts, [skip next 2 sts, work FPtr around each of next 2 sts, working in **front** of 2 sts just made, work FPtr around each o 2 skipped sts] 3 times, ★ dc in next 6 sts, [skip ne 2 sts, work FPtr around each of next 2 sts, workin in **front** of 2 sts just made, work FPtr around eacl of 2 skipped sts] 3 times; repeat from ★ 9 times **more**, dc in last 7 sts and in turning ch.

Row 80 (Celtic Diamond - fourth row)**:** Ch 2, turr skip first dc, dc in next 5 dc, [skip next 2 sts, worl BPtr around each of next 2 sts, working **behind** 2 sts just made, work BPtr around each of 2 skipp sts] 4 times, ★ dc in next 2 dc, [skip next 2 sts, work BPtr around each of next 2 sts, working **behind** 2 sts just made, work BPtr around each of 2 skipped sts] 4 times; repeat from ★ 9 times **mor** dc in last 5 dc and in turning ch.

Row 81 (Celtic Diamond - fifth row)**:** Repeat Row 79.

Row 82 (Celtic Diamond - sixth row)**:** Repeat Row 78.

Row 83 (Celtic Diamond - seventh row): Ch 2, 〔turn〕; skip first dc, dc in next 10 sts, skip next 2 sts, 〔work〕 FPtr around each of next 2 sts, working in 〔front〕 of 2 sts just made, work FPtr around each of 〔skipped sts, ★ dc in next 14 sts, skip next 2 sts, 〔work〕 FPtr around each of next 2 sts, working in 〔front〕 of 2 sts just made, work FPtr around each of 〔skipped sts; repeat from ★ 9 times **more**, dc in 〔next 11 sts and in turning ch.

Row 84 (Celtic Diamond - eighth row): Ch 1, turn; 〔do **not** skip first sc, sc in each st across and in 〔turn〕ing ch: 207 sc.

〔Cel〕tic Diamond

Rows 85-116: Repeat Rows 3-26 once, then repeat Rows 3-10 once **more**.

Rows 117-126: Repeat Rows 35-44.

Rows 127-158: Repeat Rows 3-26 once, then repeat Rows 3-10 once **more**.

Row 159: Ch 1, turn; skip first sc, sc in next sc and in each sc across, sc in turning ch; do **not** finish off.

EDGING
Ch 1, turn; slip st in each sc across; working in end of rows, sc in first row, (ch 1, sc) 101 times evenly spaced across to next corner; working in free loops of beginning ch *(Fig. 1b, page 26)*, slip st in each ch across; working in end of rows, sc in first row, (ch 1, sc) 101 times evenly spaced across; join with slip st to first st, finish off.

FRINGE
Add fringe *(Figs. 7a-c, page 27)* in first ch-1 sp and in every other ch-1 sp across each end.

GENERAL INSTRUCTIONS

ABBREVIATIONS

BPdc	Back Post double crochet(s)	hdc	half double crochet(s)
BPtr	Back Post treble crochet(s)	mm	millimeters
ch(s)	chain(s)	sc	single crochet(s)
cm	centimeters	sp(s)	space(s)
dc	double crochet(s)	st(s)	stitch(es)
FPdc	Front Post double crochet(s)	tr	treble crochet(s)
FPtr	Front Post treble crochet(s)	YO	yarn over

★ — work instructions following ★ as many **more** times as indicated in addition to the first time.

( ) or **[ ]** — work enclosed instructions **as many** times as specified by the number immediately following **or** contains explanatory remarks.

colon (:) — the number given after a colon at the end of a row or round denotes the number of stitches you should have on that row or round.

AUGE

ct gauge is essential for proper size. Before
inning your project, make the sample swatch
en in the individual instructions in the yarn
I hook specified. After completing the swatch,
asure it, counting your stitches and rows
efully. If your swatch is larger or smaller than
cified, **make another, changing hook size to
the correct gauge**. Keep trying until you find
size hook that will give you the specified gauge.
e proper gauge is obtained, measure width of
nan approximately every 3" (7.5 cm) to be sure
ge remains consistent.

Yarn Weight Symbol & Names	LACE 0	SUPER FINE 1	FINE 2	LIGHT 3	MEDIUM 4	BULKY 5	SUPER BULKY 6
Type of Yarns in Category	Fingering, 10-count crochet thread	Sock, Fingering Baby	Sport, Baby	DK, Light Worsted	Worsted, Afghan, Aran	Chunky, Craft, Rug	Bulky, Roving
Crochet Gauge* Ranges in Single Crochet to 4" (10 cm)	32-42 double crochets**	21-32 sts	16-20 sts	12-17 sts	11-14 sts	8-11 sts	5-9 sts
Advised Hook Size Range	Steel*** 6,7,8 Regular hook B-1	B-1 to E-4	E-4 to 7	7 to I-9	I-9 to K-10.5	K-10.5 to M-13	M-13 and larger

*GUIDELINES ONLY: The chart above reflects the most commonly used gauges and hook sizes for specific yarn categories.

** Lace weight yarns are usually crocheted on larger-size hooks to create lacy openwork patterns. Accordingly, a gauge range is difficult to determine. Always follow the gauge stated in your pattern.

*** Steel crochet hooks are sized differently from regular hooks–the higher the number the smaller the hook, which is the reverse of regular hook sizing.

CROCHET HOOKS

Metric mm	U.S.
2.25	B-1
2.75	C-2
3.25	D-3
3.5	E-4
3.75	F-5
4	G-6
5	H-8
5.5	I-9
6	J-10
6.5	K-10$\frac{1}{2}$
9	N
10	P
15	Q

◼◻◻◻ BEGINNER	Projects for first-time crocheters using basic stitches. Minimal shaping.
◼◼◻◻ EASY	Projects using yarn with basic stitches, repetitive stitch patterns, simple color changes, and simple shaping and finishing.
◼◼◼◻ INTERMEDIATE	Projects using a variety of techniques, such as basic lace patterns or color patterns, mid-level shaping and finishing.
◼◼◼◼ EXPERIENCED	Projects with intricate stitch patterns, techniques and dimension, such as non-repeating patterns, multi-color techniques, fine threads, small hooks, detailed shaping and refined finishing.

CROCHET TERMINOLOGY

UNITED STATES		INTERNATIONAL
slip stitch (slip st)	=	single crochet (sc)
single crochet (sc)	=	double crochet (dc)
half double crochet (hdc)	=	half treble crochet (htr)
double crochet (dc)	=	treble crochet(tr)
treble crochet (tr)	=	double treble crochet (dtr)
double treble crochet (dtr)	=	triple treble crochet (ttr)
triple treble crochet (tr tr)	=	quadruple treble crochet (qtr)
skip	=	miss

FREE LOOPS

After working in Back or Front Loops Only on a row, there will be a ridge of unused loops. These are called the free loops. Later, when instructed to work in the free loops of the same row, work in these loops (*Fig. 1a*).

Fig. 1a

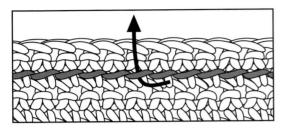

When instructed to work in free loops of a chain, work in loop indicated by arrow (*Fig. 1b*).

Fig. 1b

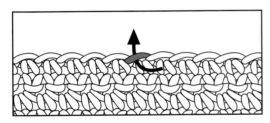

BACK OR FRONT LOOP ONLY

Work only in loop(s) indicated by arrow (*Fig. 2*).

Fig. 2

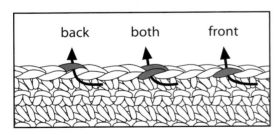

POST STITCH

Work around post of stitch indicated, inserting hook in direction of arrow (*Fig. 3*).

Fig. 3

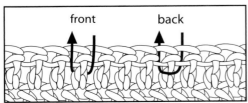

WORKING IN SPACE BEFORE A STITCH

When instructed to work in space **before** a stitch or in spaces **between** stitches, insert hook in space indicated by arrow (*Fig. 4*).

Fig. 4

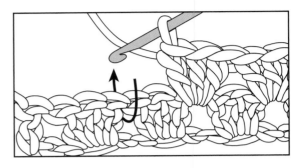

CABLE

Ch 3, skip next 2 sts, sc in next st (*Fig. 5a*), turn, sc in each ch of ch-3 just made (*Fig. 5b*), slip st in next sc (at beginning of ch-3) (*Fig. 5c*), turn, working **behind** ch-3, sc in 2 skipped sts (*Fig. 5d*).

Fig. 5a

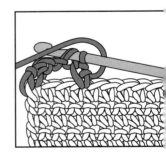

Fig. 5b

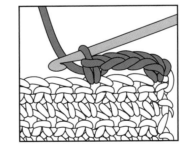

Fig. 5c

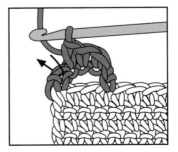

Fig. 5d

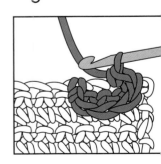

VERSE SINGLE CROCHET

(abbreviated reverse sc)

...king from **left** to **right**, ★ insert hook in st to ...t of hook *(Fig. 6a)*, YO and draw through, ...der and to left of loop on hook (2 loops on hook) ...*g. 6b)*, YO and draw through both loops on hook ...*g. 6c)* **(reverse sc made, *Fig. 6d*)**; repeat ...n ★ across.

Fig. 6a

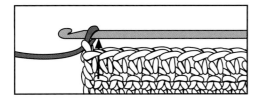

Fig. 6b

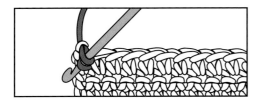

Fig. 6b

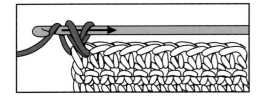

Fig. 6d

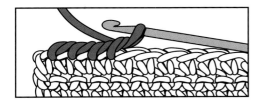

FRINGE

Cut a piece of cardboard 5" (12.5 cm) wide and 10½" (26.5 cm) long. Wind the yarn loosely and evenly lengthwise around the cardboard until the card is filled, then cut across one end; repeat as needed.

Step 1: Hold together 5 strands of yarn; fold in half. With **wrong** side facing and using a crochet hook, draw the folded end up through space specified in individual instructions and pull the loose ends through the folded end *(Fig. 7a)*; draw the knot up tightly *(Fig. 7b)*. Repeat; spacing as indicated in individual instructions.

Fig. 7a

Fig. 7b

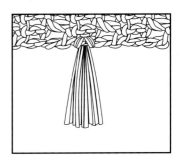

Step 2: Divide each group in half and knot together with half of next group *(Fig. 7c)*.

Fig. 7c

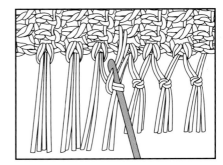

YARN INFORMATION

Each afghan in this leaflet was made using Red Heart® Super Saver® yarn. Any brand of Medium Weight Yarn may be used. It is best to refer to the yardage/meters when determining how many balls or skeins to purchase. Remember, to arrive at the finished size, it is the GAUGE/TENSION that is important, not the brand of yarn.

For your convenience, listed below are the specific yarns used to create our photography models.

Sage Green
#624 Tea Leaf

Basketweave
#313 Aran

Tan Sampler
#334 Buff

Winter White
#0150 Winter White

Autumn Orange
#254 Pumpkin

Production Team: Technical Editor – Joan Beebe; Graphic Artist – Liz Field; Photo Stylist – Sondra Daniel and Photographer – Ken West.

For digital downloads of Leisure Arts best-selling designs, visit http://www.leisureartslibrary.com